MASSACHUSETTS

A Scenic Discovery

©Copyright 1981 by Foremost Publishers, Inc.
All rights reserved.

This book, or portions thereof, may not be reproduced
in any form without permission of the publisher,
Foremost Publishers, Inc. Photographs may not be reproduced
in any form without permission of Steve Dunwell.
Edited by James B. Patrick.
Designed by Donald G. Paulhus.

Printed in Japan.
ISBN 0-89909-051-6

Published by
Foremost Publishers, Inc.
An affiliate of Yankee Publishing Inc.
Dublin, New Hampshire 03444

MASSACHUSETTS

A Scenic Discovery

Photographs and Text by Steve Dunwell

Produced by Foremost Publishers, Inc.

An affiliate of Yankee Publishing Inc.

It was with enthusiasm that I accepted a one year photographic assignment to create a book that would celebrate the authentic beauty of Massachusetts, one of the oldest states in the union. This "Scenic Discovery" assignment presented unique and exciting challenges for the creation of new images that catch the fragile and increasingly rare beauty of tradition. The mood was to be meditative and serene.

A small portion of the images shown here were the immediate reward of a first look at a new place. A few others began as peripheral glimpses. Sometimes a flash of goldenrod in an expanse of heather, or a pair of geraniums behind a farmhouse window, or a row of seagulls on a peaked roof, seen over the shoulder while cruising the highway, enticed me to stop and take a closer look. However, the majority of photographs are the fruit of detailed exploration of selected areas. When the light was not right, I made a note and returned. In this way I gradually learned the state.

The discipline of starting the day before dawn allowed me to explore Massachusetts at its most still and quiet time, when wind and temperature are at their lowest, and when the calm air transforms the landscape with dew or frost, ground fog or mist. At that time still water mirrors its surroundings most perfectly. It is a time when those few people who are up seem to be at one with their environment. Then, as day breaks, the warm glancing light embraces familiar sites, and envelops them for a brief and achingly beautiful moment; a stupendous sunrise on the eastern shore, the natural gift of the Bay State!

I began with the sea. The everchanging interplay of ocean, tide, and light on the magnificent Massachusetts coast engaged and satisfied my interest as few scenic subjects could. Again and again, patient exploration was rewarded with visual drama. By turns beguiling and hostile, the ocean remains the most primal force acting on the state.

I was entranced, too, by the seductive charm of the inland counties, by their rolling hills that culminate in the Berkshires, and by the inter-relation of nature, landscape, and society in tidy villages clustered around white frame churches beside ox-bow lakes. The intense magenta of the cranberry harvest speaks as eloquently of time, place and heritage as Plymouth Rock. Apple blossom time in Littleton and Ayer is unequaled for its sweet-smelling delicacy and visual poignancy. And throughout the state wilderness waterfalls, cutting through hemlock ledges, echo the forests cloaking the western hills. Time and time again one is reminded that this is the state where great poets, thinkers, and lovers of nature have made their homes. Indeed, "land of the Pilgrim's pride" is Massachusetts.

Through close observation I came to know the Berkshires and Boston, Cape Ann and Cape Cod, the midlands and the islands, as separate regions with individual seasonal cycles. While the magnolia herald Spring on Commonwealth Avenue, Canadian geese are breeding on Plum Island. Summer heat raises billowing cumulus clouds over Lenox pastures and lowers impenetrable fog on Marblehead. A bumper crop of South Shore cranberries and the frost underfoot in Williamstown both foretell Autumn. Winter brings utter stillness to Wachusett forests in snow and hurls its storm breakers against Cape Cod shores, while we await the thaw.

Having explored Massachusetts and made it my home, I have come to love it. And I hope that these photographs show to all who see them that this is a very special place, animated at once by the delicate and traditional rhythms of its land and people, and by the strong tides and currents of nature. This state deserves our respect.

Boston   Steve Dunwell
April, 1979